HEALTHY
TOMORROWS,
FEED
YOUR MIND,
TRANSFORM
YOUR BODY,
RESHAPE
YOUR LIFE
...one day at a time

Elizabeth Sellars CNP, RNCP

BALBOA.PRESS

A DIVISION OF HAY HOUSE

Balboa Press books may be ordered through booksellers or by contacting:

Balboa Press
A Division of Hay House
1663 Liberty Drive
Bloomington, IN 47403
www.balboapress.com
844-682-1282

Because of the dynamic nature of the Internet, any web addresses or
links contained in this book may have changed since publication and
may no longer be valid. The views expressed in this work are solely those
of the author and do not necessarily reflect the views of the publisher,
and the publisher hereby disclaims any responsibility for them.

The author of this book does not dispense medical advice or prescribe
the use of any technique as a form of treatment for physical, emotional,
or medical problems without the advice of a physician, either directly
or indirectly. The intent of the author is only to offer information
of a general nature to help you in your quest for emotional and
spiritual well-being. In the event you use any of the information in
this book for yourself, which is your constitutional right, the author
and the publisher assume no responsibility for your actions.

Any people depicted in stock imagery provided by Getty Images are
models, and such images are being used for illustrative purposes only.
Certain stock imagery © Getty Images.

Print information available on the last page.

ISBN: 978-1-9822-5163-5 (sc)
ISBN: 978-1-9822-5164-2 (e)

Balboa Press rev. date: 09/29/2020

CONTENTS

CHAPTER 1

Present Moment Awareness

Habit is habit and not to be flung out the window by any man but coaxed downstairs one step at a time.
—Mark Twain

Forget about your New Year's resolutions, which you decide on every first day of January regarding how you will conduct your life for the next twelve months. Instead, set up day-to-day goals for yourself, and then resolve to begin living with present-moment awareness... one day at a time. You'll see yourself changing right before your own surprised eyes.

Remember, anyone can do anything for just one day, so tune out the sentences that keep you locked into your self-defeating ways and begin your transformation, one day at a time.

Living with present-moment awareness means being mindful of how and what you are thinking. This is an important foundation to know, and is the basis of this book. Being aware brings about enlightenment: it comes from "knowing who you truly are."

This may be a new concept for you, but the fact is that you are a spiritual being having a human experience, not the other way around. We are here to evolve, to raise consciousness, and to be filled with love and wisdom. Life is like a classroom where you learn and grow and share your experiences with other human beings. It's like a spiritual school, and each life experience is like one academic year. I feel like we are operating at kindergarten level and are not truly aware of what is going on here. In a way, we are ignorant of this fact and must learn to turn our ignorance into wisdom.

There are 12 Laws of the Universe, and practicing them can give us this foundation we need to grow and to have a better understanding of why we are all here and how it all works. They will help us become more aware; and like faith, they can lead us to that place of joy, peace and wisdom. They will show us not only how to apply these principles for losing weight, but how to create anything else you want to achieve in your life. We are going to explore your depth of understanding. Your true nature.

THE 12 LAWS OF THE UNIVERSE

1. **LAW OF ONENESS** - This law states that everything is connected to one source. We are a source of energy. We are spiritual beings having a human experience. Everything we think and do has an effect on the collective and the entire universe. So be aware of what you think about as our thoughts are the most powerful form of energy. You can power or disempower yourself just by your thoughts. We are capable of becoming telepathic.

2. **LAW OF VIBRATION** - Everything is energy and energy moves and vibrates at different frequencies. This must be understood and is evident in every aspect of your life. It is going to depend on what you attract in your life... high vibration feeling good... low vibration not so good. A walk in nature is a good example of high vibration. Go in the direction in life to

what feels good... another example is to do what you love so you will never have to work again. Be aware and listen to your inner guidance system. Living in a conditioned society we tend to forget or ignore what makes us feel good.

3. **LAW OF CORRESPONDENCE** - Your reality will always reflect your inner beliefs... if we want to see change we must first start with "the man in the mirror "our inner beliefs.

4. **LAW OF ATTRACTION** - This law states that like attracts like. You can use this law of attraction to bring better health into your life, an example of this is to be grateful, ask for healing, picture yourself strong, healthy and visualize your cells functioning at optimal health.

5. **LAW OF INSPIRED ACTION** - Taking steps toward <u>what you want</u>, whether it is a job, a relationship or weight loss.

This action comes from following your inner guidance system, following your heart. It is a knowing, a feeling that you are doing the right thing. This is where creativity lies.

6. **LAW OF TRANSMUTATION OF ENERGY** - This law means that you can redirect your energies, so if you find yourself surrounded by a negative energy know that you can redirect it in a more positive direction. Energy cannot be created or destroyed but can be transmuted. Know you can change the channel, and that you are in control.

7. **LAW OF CAUSE AND EFFECT** - Creating negative or positive reactions. This law is based on the Law of Attraction... what you send out you get back. When you offer a positive vibe you get a positive reaction. When you marry your head (electrical energy) with your heart (magnetic energy) you can create what you want.

8. **LAW OF COMPENSATION** - You reap what you sow...giving

9. **LAW OF RELATIVITY** - Everything is relative; looking at things from a different perspective can make you more grateful. Life changes are stepping stones. They represent a challenge for the soul.

10. **LAW OF POLARITY** - Everything has an opposite.

11. **LAW OF RHYTHM** - All things come in cycles or seasons, and nothing lasts forever.

12. **LAW OF GENDER** – Yin and yang; we must find a balance

So you see, everything is connected, and everything is energy. Your thoughts are the most powerful form of energy, which are all orchestrated by the Law of Attraction. This law is relevant because when you are focused on losing weight, you must continually have to lose weight; your thoughts attract like energies. The condition of losing weight was created by you thinking of it. Simply put, if someone is overweight, it comes from them thinking 'fat' thoughts, whether that person was aware of it or not. Thinking 'thin' thoughts and being fat definitely defines the Law of Attraction. Positive thoughts create high energy and fast metabolism; negative thoughts create low energy and slow metabolism. When your vibration shifts to positive thoughts around food, your weight will decrease, so it is important to make peace where you are. Our body is a reflection of ourselves and what we believe (or what we think).

Being aware of nutrition and moving your body is helpful, but this mind-body connection is the most important factor. Here is the proof. Have you ever considered why some people can eat whatever they want and never gain weight? It's because of their relationship with food, and the energy balance in their bodies. I cannot stress it enough: how you feel and what you think matters. Your thoughts do create your life, not only with regard to food, but to anything else you want to change in your life. Once you realize this, you can create a whole new world of possibilities.

Understand the power of your thoughts and you will look forward to seeing the physical changes in your body which reflect the changes in your thinking, one day at a time. If your thinking does not change, then even if you lose weight, you'll retain an overwhelming subconscious urge to gain it back. Expanding your awareness will dissolve these old patterns. How quickly you lose weight would become less important; what would be important is how holistically you lose weight. You want your mind, your emotions and your body to all lose weight: that which disappears from your body but not from your soul is simply being recycled. It is almost certain to return. It's self-defeating; therefore, you will struggle to drop the excess weight unless you are also willing to drop the thought forms that initially produced it and now hold it in place.

In this book, you will be feeding your mind with powerful thoughts every day; and transforming your body will be its natural side effect. You will be going with the flow. Trying hard points upstream; it's low vibrational energy. When you go with the flow, you raise your vibration and start feeling motivated. This is called inspiration, or being inspired from the inside out (universal law #5). Celebrate food, and declare it your friend. Believe it! There is no vibrational variance than it is. Remember, every part of your awareness around food is vibrational; food is vibrational. You will transform your body by creating this awareness.

There is a whole area of psychology concerned with cultivating a greater awareness in eating and the behavior associated with it, such as reading labels, controlling portion sizes, a person's eating speed, social connections and pressures, snacking, and unconscious and unexamined thoughts but these powerful emotions related to food and eating are what's most important. Feeling bad about yourself will cause emotional eating and lower your vibration and metabolism.

Losing weight with the proper foundation and beliefs will guarantee your success, so stay focused on the solution and think about what you are going to gain by losing weight. To make it real, you must align your daily actions with your intention to lose weight.

You must be an energetic match for what you are seeking, so act as if you've already manifested it. Think and act like the thin person you want to be!

To lose weight successfully, you must also know and feel in your heart that you can do it. You must see yourself as capable of achieving your goal. You can also use some of the affirmations in this book as your mantras. This will help you believe you can accomplish your goal.

Your beliefs create a self-fulfilling prophecy as you manifest them outward and create your reality.

The wisest book ever written, the *Tao Te Ching*, teaches us that when we have a surplus, reduce; and when we have deficiencies, increase. This is also a way to create balance. Verse 33 says: "He who knows he has enough is rich." In order to bring this into perspective, we must bring in the inner you: what you are seeking is the perfect balance between you and you since not having enough is EGO, which comes from the physical realm. You are not that needy entity that says "I want more"; your answers come from within. Remember, anyone can do anything for just one day, so tune out the sentences that keep you locked into your self-defeating ways and begin your transformation. Greatness arises out of small things, out of that first step. Honor each step into this moment.

The following chapter contains your daily practice, which will feed your mind and transform your body, ...one day at a time.

I am Grateful

_____

_____

_____

_____

_____

_____

_____

_____

_____

_____

_____

_____

_____

My Dreams

_____

_____

_____

_____

_____

_____

_____

_____

_____

_____

_____

_____

_____

CHAPTER 2

30 Day Transformation

DAY 1 (Monday)

Feed Your Mind

> *A journey of a thousand miles*
> *begins with the first step.*
> *— Lao Tzu*

Transform Your Body

Step 1: Appreciation

When you wake up each morning, write down the 10 things you are grateful for.

Then repeatedly say "Thank you, thank you, thank you."

Appreciation is the best way to bring more of what you already have into your experience. It is the highest form of vibration!

Step 2: Meditation

Start by sitting in a quiet place. Then ask yourself the following questions (repeat these over and over until you get answers):

Mantra

Who am I?

What do I want? (knowing you have a choice)

what is my life's purpose?

Go back to times when you experienced joy, your deepest desires and meditate on this. Think back and observe .Travel back to early times where you had a strong feeling as to how you wanted to express yourself. What was resonating ...what said to you "this is it" "this is what I want to do". Remember how you saw it? How you felt it? That is what you were born to express, this is what you have come here to do.

So keep repeating this meditation .It is your mantra... if you are distracted, keep focusing on your words. Set a timer for 10 minutes. Keep asking until you get answers; these will come from within you.

Meditation creates that awareness within you and releases who you really are, your true essence. We are beings of love and light. God said, "Let there be light." Light is a high vibration of positive energy. It is built into us. We are all made in His image, just as Jesus was enlightened by Him so we too can be enlightened... We are all a piece of the divine. This knowledge is super important and truly your foundation from which to grow... with this realization you will not only release the weight, synchronicity's will begin to happen and your dreams will begin to manifest. All you have to do is know "who you really are" and what you want. Most of all, believe that it can happen! This step is very important;

knowing what you want is the key, and where you will find your purpose!

Step 3: Signs

Before falling to sleep think about the best thing that happened to you during the day. Be aware of the signs that the universe has brought you, and be grateful for knowing about them. Say "Thank you." You can also connect by praying....... Most importantly listening to your affirmations will reprogram your subconscious mind.

Remember, you will alter your life in the most powerful way; you will reach your goals, experience a life of happiness, a feeling of confidence, creating what you love with great success, of more abundance than you could ever imagine and with much joy and bliss... Welcome to Paradise... it just takes 3 small steps each day for 30 days......... your choice!

DAY 2 (Tuesday)

Feed Your Mind

There is a spiritual solution to every problem. To have a new body, you must be willing to have a new perspective to give rise to new solutions.

Step 1: Morning Appreciation

Write down or repeat out loud for that which you are grateful. Do this first thing in the morning.

Step 2: Meditation

A shift in awareness is the first change you'll make. Set a timer for 10 minutes, once again repeat the following:

Mantra

Who am I?

What do I want?

What is my purpose?

Ask yourself if you are still breathing. Your sensory receptors will bring you into the present.

Step 3: Evening Reflection

While lying in bed, think about the best thing that happened to you during the day. Be aware of the signs that the universe has placed before you. These are all clues. Then give thanks. Listen to your affirmations before sleep. Also, be aware of your dreams. They will guide you toward what you want.

DAY 3 (Wednesday)

Feed Your Mind

Create your own life. If you have faith and not doubt, not only can you do what was done to the fig tree, you can say to this mountain, "Move from here to there" and it will move. Nothing will be impossible for you.

Transform Your Body

Step 1: Appreciation

Write down or repeat out loud 10 things you are grateful for.

These are insights from the universe, which is speaking to you. It is your inner voice. Then continue write down the 10 things you are grateful for. Say "Thank you."

Step 2: Meditation

The more aware you become of your spiritual being, the more you'll want to respect your physical being. It's spiritual when you love yourself too much to eat foods that do not nourish your body.

This morning, try talking to the universe. Tell it what you want; ask, and it is given. If you find yourself not quite knowing what you want, repeat your mantra again. Focus on these words:

Who am I?

What do I want?

What is my purpose?

Include here your daily practice, whether it be yoga, walking or any type of exercise that helps you feel good!

Step 3: Signs

Once again while lying in bed, think about the best thing that happened to you during the day. Say "Thank you" to the universe. Listen to your affirmations......Sweet dreams! Look for any signs that might be a result of your dream state, think about how they relate to your own life, think about what they are saying.

DAY 4 (Thursday)

Feed Your Mind

If you want to see what your thoughts were like yesterday, look at your body today. If you want to see what your body will look like tomorrow, look at your thoughts today.

Transform Your body

Step 1: Appreciation

Write down 10 things you are grateful for. Do not skip this as there is something magical that flows from your hand to the paper that enters the mind, body and spirit

Also the words you speak are very powerful. Here is an affirmation I like to say .I will list more in this book

"I am open to oneness, to cosmo peace, joy, creativity, health and unconditional love. I am grateful, grateful, grateful."

Also write down your dreams and take note of how they relate to your own life.

Step 2 : Meditation

Set your clock for 10 minutes.

Repeat once again

Who am I?

What do I want?

What is my purpose?

Stay focused on these questions and the answer will come.

Step 3: Signs

Once again, just before you fall asleep, think about the best things that happened to you during the day, and be grateful for them. Reprogram your mind by listening to your affirmations or repeat. …" I am open to oneness, to cosmic peace, joy, creativity, health and unconditional love."

DAY 5 (Friday)

Feed Your Mind

To make your dreams come true, you must go to the unseen world of the spirit or inspiration that will guide you to anything you would like to have in your life.

Transform Your Body

Step 1: Appreciation

Upon awakening write down your dreams. From now on, be aware of them. Then write down 10 things you are grateful for . You can even be grateful for your dreams. Repeatedly say "Thank you, thank you, thank you."

Step 2: Meditation or Prayer

If we can smile and be peaceful and happy in our daily life, everyone will benefit from it. This is the most basic kind of peace work.

Silence is a great teacher; and to learn its lesson, you must pay attention. There are no substitutes for the creative inspiration, knowledge and stability that come from knowing how to contact your core of inner silence.

Set your timer for 10 minutes, and repeat your mantra. Talk to the universe. You will be surprised by what happens.

Who am I?

What do I want?

What is my purpose?

Step 3: Signs

Before going to sleep, think about the best thing that happened to you during the day. Look for signs, and thank the universe. Listen to affirmations once again before sleep to reprogram your mind.

DAY 6 (Saturday)

Feed Your Mind

In every second of your existence, you are creating a new body. A quiet mind is all you need.

Transform Your Body

Step 1: Appreciation

After waking up, write down the 10 things you are grateful for. Speak the words "Thank you, thank you, thank you." Remember to write down your dreams and look for the meaning of them in your own life.

Step 2: Meditation

Do this for 10 minutes. Ask the following questions:

Who am I?

What do I want?

What is my purpose?

Step 3: Signs

As your head touches your pillow, think about the things that happened to you during the day; and pay attention to the signs. Think positive uplifting thoughts or listen to your affirmations.

DAY 7 (Sunday)

Feed Your Mind

The biochemistry of theory is the product of awareness, beliefs, thoughts and emotions that create the chemical reactions that uphold life in every cell. All things are possible to those who believe. Your body is mostly a reflection of the thoughts you think. The rest are small and subtle changes that make food your friend.

Transform Your Body

Step 1: Appreciation

First thing in the morning, write down in your book the 10 things that you are grateful for. Say "Thank you, thank you, thank you."....don't forget your dreams!

Step 2: Meditation

Sit quiet for the last day of the week . It is Sunday.... a day of rest.

Ask yourself the following questions:

Who am I?

What do I want?

What is my purpose?

Take it one step at a time. Include a daily exercise practice to raise your vibration.

This is how I answered these three questions.

Who am I ...I am a child of the stars, I am a piece of the creator.

What do I want? .....I want to write, paint, dance, listen to music, go on adventures, explore the outdoors, grow my own food, build my own little house and live sustainability .I would like a partner of the same mind set.

Step 3: Signs

Before sleeping, think about what you are grateful for; did you know that by doing this more will come to you... of course you did... it is the Law of Attraction. Sweet dreams!

Congratulations! You have finished week 1. By now, you should be feeling different. Carry on and you will see yourself changing right before your own surprised eyes. You will have a lot to write down and be thankful for and also as you become aware of the meaning of your dreams and what they mean, how they relate and how they can literally create and manifest the life of your dreams.

CHAPTER 3

Supplements

As a Registered Holistic Nutritionist, I have spent many years helping people achieve optimal health through diet and lifestyle changes. But what always got my attention the most was a person's lifestyle and how this related to their well-being. I looked at the family history, their attitudes, their job, their relationships with others, etc. What I discovered was that their attitudes and how they reacted to life situations were imperative to their health. Those whose minds wandered in the past and future experienced a great deal of stress, resulting in declining health. We now know that this way of thinking penetrates in the body, causing blocked energy and disease. Remember, we are energy; and our thoughts are a powerful form of energy, with all thoughts orchestrated by the Law of Attraction. We get what we think about.

Think of your body as your temple. Remember that you are a piece of the divine, and it is your responsibility to take care of it. Get in touch with it, love it, have an appreciation of yourself. Develop self-worth and cut the cords that connect you to people who do not serve you and do not appreciate you. Be aware of how you spend your time, and what choices you make. Learn to be alone because the truth is that you are never alone. I remember Wayne Dyer saying the following and I never forgot it "if you knew who walked beside you on this path that you have chosen you would never experience fear or doubt again" There are only two emotions, love and fear. The more you like and love yourself, the more your body will say, "Finally, you get it." You are connected! Insights and premonitions will follow.

Walking and hydrating your body will help it function at its peak. There are 5 nutritional supplements that are a must for general maintenance, and help keep the body's energy functions flowing: enzymes, probiotics, fiber, oils, and vitamins and minerals (greens). Get plenty of sunshine (vitamin D). Do not hide from the sun. It is a source of well-being and intelligence. It is light and carries gamma waves of intelligence. Contrary to popular belief, do not use sunscreen. It will contribute to skin diseases. Just practice common sense; stay out of the sun during the hottest time of the day so you do not burn, and wear long-sleeved shirts. You are along for the ride when it comes to your body. Start loving it. Have loving, loyal, and tender sexual experiences. It is very healing. It will improve your overall functioning and well-being. We have all come here for love. Love your body because everything works. What a miracle, a precious gift from the divine!

Picture the type of body you want. Believe it, and you will see it! It is law!

CHAPTER 4

Ayurveda and the Mind Body Connection

Now let's take a closer look at this mind-body connection, which comes from 5,000-year-old Ayurvedic medicine. It helped me understand how our emotions are related to our state of health. It is also regarded as our tool for our spiritual growth. We have to be aware of and in tune with what is happening on the inside as well as the outside. This is healing from the inside out.

This teaching takes into consideration the relationship between individual spirit and cosmic spirit, individual consciousness and cosmic consciousness, energy and matter. It is based on our awareness and understanding of how these tools or feelings play an important role in one's health. Understand that we are vibrational beings; so with regard to food, "how we feel about it" plays a role in determining our weight. Some foods also have a higher frequency than others, and eating them while feeling good greatly enhances the level of consciousness and lends power to intention.

Below are the most important foods and thoughts to consider to help raise consciousness:

Raw foods -These foods cleanse your senses and turn you into a powerful broadcaster of intention.

Vegetarian foods -Also cleanse the body and raise vibration.

Personal Integrity -Acting with integrity multiplies your power of intention. I will speak more of this in the next chapter.

Superfoods/Herbs -They cleanse the liver, purify the blood, and improve mental clarity.

Healthy fats -These make a big difference on the power and reach of your intention. Choose chia seeds, avocados, raw coconut oil, and plant-based oils. Fish oils can also be supportive if you choose to eat fish-derived products. Flax seeds serve a similar purpose for vegetarians.

Berries -Eat big amounts of raw berries. They are a major antioxidant.

Our diets will change as we evolve.

Below are more ways to enhance your power of intention and raise vibration:

(Appreciation, Meditation and Gratefulness are at the top of this list)

Essential oils - Diffusing, topical

Grounding - Walking barefoot

Deep Breathing - Keeps you in the present moment

Candles - Focusing on the light

Music - Sound and notes raise frequency

Laughter - Keeps energy flowing

Sleep - Rejuvenates

Massage - Power of touch

Hugs - Love

Sex - Present moment - higher dimension

Bach Flowers - Inhaling smell

Homeopathy - Raises energy, unblocks blocked energy

Tuning Forks - Pitch raises vibration

Visualization - Believe it and you will see it!

Rock crystals - Contain energy

Flowers - Unfolding of energy

Water - Life force.

Once you align with you, you will gravitate toward the foods and other tools that are good for you. You will become aware of your thoughts and your actions. Allow yourself to be guided. You are looking for balance and harmony in all things. A variety of different energies provide that balance.

Your daily practise of meditation staying in the present moment and talking to the universe, saying what you want, and being grateful for what you have will help you stay guided. Remember, healthy people live neither in the past nor in the future; they live in the present, the now. This is where you'll find the inner joyfulness that should be yours all the time.

This 30-day meditation training has brought you to a clear and calm center of your being. No matter what is happening in your outer world, you can always return to this sanctuary of the soul, where peace, love, happiness and joyfulness are states that live within you.

CHAPTER 5

Affirmations and Quotes

There is only one stream: the stream of goodness and wellness. Do not pinch yourself off. Speak of what you want, not want you do not want – the universe does not know no. Nothing you want is upstream. If you try and fight the current, the stream will beat you up. Stop looking at what is there and start looking at creating what you want! Go with the flow; stop going upstream. Every illness is about your relationship with your stream. You have a built-in guidance system:

Feel good - Good match

Feel bad - Bad match

When you feel negative emotion, you separate yourself from who you are. If the belly is good, all is normal.

The following affirmations and quotes will help keep you on track. Remember, what goes in will not define you, but what comes out of your mouth will. Universal Law # 3 (the Law of Oneness), so the words you speak and the choices you make affect your energy flow but also your thoughts affect others and the collective consciousness. The following affirmations will empower you!

Affirmations

I am growing more powerful with every storm I endure.

I am beautiful and capable of greatness.

It is my time to shine in divine glory.

I am guided and supported by the clarity of vision of my true nature.

I am joyful.

I am happy.

My body is perfect the way it is, and I honor it in this state.

I am comfortable in my own skin.

I am divinely guided.

I am awake.

I am source energy.

I am blessed.

I am worthy.

I am beautiful.

I am flowing.

I am powerful.

I am focused.

I am grace.

I am kind.

I am imaginative.

I am in harmony.

I am well-being.

I am inspired.

I am playful.

I am at peace.

I am vital.

I am spirit.

I am light.

I am eternal.

I am in love.

I am that I am.

Quotes

Change from seeing yourself disconnected to everyone and everything in the universe to seeing yourself as connected to them.

New beginnings are disguised as painful endings.

No storm lasts forever.

Knowing others is wisdom. Knowing yourself is enlightenment.

You should not run away from your problems. You should aim straight for the heart of the beast.

Knowledge is learning something every day. Wisdom is letting go of something every day.

We must be willing to let go of the life that we planned to accept the life that is waiting for us.

It's the company, not the cooking, that makes a meal.

It does not matter how slowly you go as long as you do not stop.

Whatever is happening is a vibrational indicator of your attraction.

Circumstances do not matter. Only the state of being matters.

It never hurts to see the good in someone. They act better because of it. - Nelson Mandela

Follow your bliss. - Joseph Campbell

We are living in exciting times. We find ourselves learning new concepts and reaching higher levels (graduating from kindergarten).We are becoming mindful of paying <u>attention to the right things and not paying attention to the wrong things.</u> We are now focusing on what we do want and are aware of what we say and what we speak. Learning these new displients is bringing us to higher consciousness. The thoughts we choose to think are the tools we use to paint the canvas of our lives.

CHAPTER 6

Exercise

You have been practicing being aware of what you are eating and what you are thinking. You are feeding your mind transforming your body one **day at a time**. Now you want to maintain peak performance. Remember your body is your vehicle of operation.... your temple.

Think of it as your car, it will run more smoothly with general maintenance. Along with the foods you eat, there are also forms of movement that help your body operate at peak performance. Walking is a favorite, and so is yoga. My favorite type of yoga is hatha yoga. This style focuses on holding your posture; this is what gives you strength. You will find that it also makes you feel good and gives you courage, discipline, clarity and "mindfulness"; losing weight and getting in shape will be natural side effects.

Go to YouTube www.health and beauty.com and enter my virtual studio. Even if you start with just a couple of poses, that would be great. Remember, take it **one day at a time.** Little by little does it every time. Once you know these poses, you can do them anywhere and anytime. You will feel good, and feeling good will raise your vibration.

Yoga also helps us take time out. Remember that most of us take for granted that time flies meaning that it passes too quickly but in the mindful state time does not really pass at all.... there is only a single instant of time that keeps renewing itself over and over with infinite variety. Follow this and you will never grow old; you will just pass through time. Here lies beauty and dignity.

CHAPTER 7

A Shift in Humanity

I believe there is a shift is taking place around the world as many are realizing that the old paradigm is not working. In time as more and more become enlightened we will shift humanity into a higher consciousness and create a better life for all people. Did you know that one enlightened person is more powerful than the millions who are not.! This just keeps better and better!

Over time, people will experience more psychic abilities. More healing and miracles will happen. New thinking will change the world, and will be known as cosmic intelligence. We will create more positive energy in favor of light by healing and raising our vibration. Now, we are also healing our past and future selves. All healing can be facilitated through this love and forgiveness. We are changing new energies for the new world. We are here to create the new energy of love and light so we can have heaven on earth, both for future generations and ourselves.

My vision of heaven on earth is to create a world where people are free to grow, learn and experience joy and freedom. The energy we create inside ourselves will have a direct impact on the world. The old energies of control create non-consent in equality and imbalance. Our higher consciousness is needed to change racism, social classes, poverty, debt, and the imbalance of resources and greed (such as cannabis and hemp, for example); have a border-free world so people can move about freely; as well as control slavery through TV, politics, human trafficking and survival issues, animals and animal rights and human rights and assistance for people who need to achieve personal growth to provide them with empowerment and self-esteem that encourages growth and productivity and focuses on the **harmonious balance of life on our planet.**

We are becoming more aware of all of this through higher consciousness. I know now we are not alone. I know we each have our own guardian angel. When we change the way we see these things, change the way we think about ourselves, anything is possible. So you see, this little book is not just about weight loss, it's about discovering a whole new world ,reshaping a whole new life with a knowing that you can change and create anything you want .Why not focus on that and transform your time here on earth into something wonderful and more meaningful!

Meditate on what you want. You now know the power of silence. You now know you can be in control. You now know you are the creator of your own experience. Focus on what you want and how you want your life to be, and it will be so.

You have to know who you are and train yourself to expand, even though science tries to convince you otherwise. Science and its conclusions are one-dimensional, and there it's greatest limitations. Thus, it will never supersede what humans already know.

Don't wait for them to catch up. You now know you are not only in control of your weight, but you can reshape your whole life. Your body responds to your thoughts, and attaining your perfect weight is a natural side effect of well-being, just as our freedom and growth are natural. Don't dance around the perimeter of who you are here to be; dive in and own your power!

CHAPTER 8

Our Greatest Treasure

My intention was to finish at chapter 7 but apparently the universe had other plans. There is so much more now to write about... so much more is happening on this planet. I find myself, very quickly in the mist of what seems like a crazy time in the here and now. I find myself in the middle of an upheaval but I understood somewhere deep within me that everything is going to be ok. I understand the power we have within us and I understand the power of the universe. I am fully aware that in order to transform and bring forth a new there is going to be upheaval. Remember when you tore down your old kitchen cupboards and redecorated how beautiful the finished product looked? Let's focus on that analogy and know there is a reason for everything or as my mother used to say "it will all work out in the wash".

I believe this book now will not only Feed your Mind, Transform your Body...it will Reshape your Life, so I have added that to the title. Our life is reshaping right in front of us. Out of the upheaval comes the reshaping. You are about truth and integrity, taking care of this planet and recognizing that we are all connected. Our higher consciousness is understanding all this now. It is only through this diversity that we evolve. We are reaching higher consciousness and seeing the truth and because of this lower consciousness is being exposed... if you had to take one lesson home from this little daily guide book I hope it will be to know "who you truly are" and the power you have within to change yourself and the world.

There is much more good news. We are going to tell a new story. As we grow in this consciousness we are going to see many changes on this planet. In just three months I have witnessed the whole world change right before my eyes. It is ironic that I am writing this on Canada Day, a day when we traditionally celebrate this great country. We sing the national anthem with the words glorious and free.... well people are finally waking up to the fact that it may not be so glorious and free. They are not willing to go along with what is happening. We are finally saying NO. They want to tell a new story and envision a new world of harmony and peace.

Yes it may appear to those who have not awakened as if we have seriously stumbled but here lies our greatest treasure NOW... out of all this chaos comes the great awakening!!! YES more and more people are waking up to the truth to what is really going on. For over 2000 years we have been under this spell where there was separateness, wars and millions of people were killed. Finally after all this time more and more people are coming together recognizing we are one and discovering the power of love. Remember one person who is enlightened is more powerful than millions who are not. It is a very exciting time to be alive to be witnessing the likes of which we may never witness again. I feel this shutdown has given people time to regroup. They are starting to think for themselves, they are finding new ways to reinvent themselves, to be more self sufficient, more creative. This way of thinking is bringing a more peaceful and harmonious world. This is changing not only how we perceive the world, how we conduct our lives, how we choose the foods we eat but also how we heal our bodies... yes underneath all this is a beautifully hidden treasure. It brings more of us to higher consciousness! Now as I reach out and apply this higher consciousness I cannot help but think we are not alone. I find myself looking up more and more and wanting that connection with my star family. In 1929 scientists told us there was only one galaxy, the Milky Way and thanks to awareness and Quantum Physics we now know there are billions of galaxies! This is exciting news and is opening up the cosmo's for exploration. I know I will be exploring! The way I see it if there are billions of galaxies it just makes sense to me that there must be other species as well. To date I have studied one species, The Pleiadians. I believe they are helping us reach higher consciousness .I believe it is time now to hear a new story. I found out they are from the star cluster The Pleiades and have evolved millions of years ago .They are the early races of mankind....of us! They are intensely spiritual and loving, they are healers, understand creativity, musical, nurturing,intuitive,empathic, radiant, sensitive and are tuned into nature. I am mindful of this and understand that they act with integrity and are teaching us to do the same. I have written their teachings on the next page. I have enlarged the print, just as I did with (The Laws of the Universe,), as you may want to display it in your home as a reminder of how integrity can raise your Power of Intention.

Pleiadian Teachings

1. Don't hurt

2. Be an honorable being and express a noble character in all your behaviour

3. Practise self searching so you get mastery of yourself

4. Take responsibility for yourself so you do not depend on anyone

5. Be the highest version of yourself

6. A Sovereign assumes complete responsibility of their own life

7. Sovereign Beings live fully and do not require any authority, Gods or teachers

8. A Sovereign Being does what he or she desires

9. Sovereign Beings do not manipulate, deceive or control and do not allow anyone to master him or her in any way.

10. Sovereign Beings keep their word and fulfill all contracts he or she has validated with their honor

11. Sovereign is a realization of what and who is real

12. Sovereign believes there is no less than God

This shift is not only helping us become aware of ourselves and how we treat others; this light energy and higher consciousness is also changing our DNA and as a result we are becoming lighter beings. We will begin to gravitate towards lighter, higher vibrational foods. These foods will not only give more energy but will help us live longer, look more radiant, slender and more angelic. What a great thing to stumble upon! We are obviously evolving. I have listed these foods in Chapter 4 of this book. You can choose what food is best for you. Ayurveda body typing is a good place to start and based on the energetic field of the body. You can learn more by going to my blog at www. healthytomorrows.club. Looking at health from a physical point of view is only going to take you so far, you have to look at the body from an energetic point of view. The truth is we attract to us what our frequency desires for instance lighter foods my bring forth emotional issues that we may not be ready to look at so we eat what we call comfort foods instead. This indicates you are not ready to deal with these emotions. You are not going to let the physical body lighten up. In this situation you need to look at your life, your relationships etc. You cannot separate the two. When you are ready to raise your consciousness, then and only then will you be ready to eat lighter foods.

You can release these emotions by repro-gramming your subconscious mind. If you go back to your daily practice those few minutes before you fall to sleep are going to will do just that. So think about the best thing that happened to you that day and repeat to yourself the affirmations or listen to mediation before you drift off to sleep. Following this simple step can make all the difference in the world and reset your mind as you drift off to sleep there is part of your brain that turns off the conscious mind and drifts into the part of the brain that is still operating in the subconscious mind . Ask the creator for what you want... he will give you the answers. Remember to study the Laws of the Universe and the Pleiadian Teachings... These will guide you. I have them both framed. This is a new model of how to live your life with awareness, knowledge, peace and freedom!

Did you know your subconscious mind also plays a large role in your overall health? For instance low vibrational thoughts such as hate are correlated to colon cancer.. It is powerful and can go either way.... your choice. This is a planet of free choice and free will. You are the one who is supposed to be in control! Many of our beliefs have been formed before the age of seven. Our earlier experiences and understandings develop a series of beliefs that have been used to create your life up until now. 90% of the population thinks they are not good enough, not worthy. This all stems from not knowing who they truly are. Erkart Tolle said it right... the first lesson children should be taught in school is "Who am I?. Some day I believe it will! It is imperative to have a foundation from which to grow .Once you know who it is you truly are you will be able to change your life by using your own mental powers and taking control of your mind, This is how you will reshape your life. Practise each day, open your eyes and know what is possible! So you see this little book is about something bigger. It is about shifting and reshaping your whole life. Let's realign back to our spiritual nature. The entire universe has our attention at this time teaching us the truth.... all we have to do is listen .By doing so we are not only reaching higher consciousness we are bringing with it more possibilities than we could ever imagine. Many people have figured this out and stumbled upon this great gift of "knowing who we truly are"!!!!!!...... there lies our greatest treasure.!!!!

ACKNOWLEDGEMENTS

I grew up with a heavy christian influence and my faith was as much a part of my life as my home and school. My uncle lived with the family and was the organist and choir director at church and my music teacher and at school. Despite being in the middle with three sisters and one older brother I had a knowing that "all things are possible for those that believe".

My mother served as a nurse and my father was a captain who sailed big ships in the North Atlantic. I remember that he had to leave on some Christmases and go out to sea. But before he would leave, he would wrap parcels for the poor. I recall him saying that the closest time he felt to God was during early-morning watch in the open sea. He didn't go to church with us that often, but picked vegetables from his garden and prepared a roast beef dinner that we all looked forward to enjoying after church.

I am glad I had that experience and guidance from my parents and my uncle, **who taught me about faith, kindness, courage and compassion. Without them, I would not have been able to write this book.**

A short while before my mother made her transition, my sister took a picture of a beautiful monarch butterfly that landed on her lap while she was visiting my father's birthplace in Newfoundland. She had truly transformed, and so had I.

This book is about transformation. We are all transforming in different ways each and every day. It is part of our evolution. I have included this picture in this book, and dressed the front cover with the monarch butterfly's beauty as a symbol of transformation.

We have evolved from the 5,000-year-old Ayurvedic philosophy to our present awareness of time and space! We now know we can create our own reality!

Enlightenment is real. Each of us, in the right circumstances and with the right training, can realize the nature of the mind; and so know in ourselves what is deathless and eternally pure.

We are paving the way for future generations, just as the older generations have helped us.

Science will never supersede what humans already know about themselves.

There is a reason why science has a naive understanding of ourselves and the universe: **it can only discover correlations, not causation**. It does not have a concept of quantum measurements. It has no tools to measure quantum fields. Since everything in the universe happens at a quantum level, science as we know it is only able to teach concepts starting from how relationships function, but not why those relationships exist. Science and its conclusions are **one-dimensional**, and there lies its greatest limitations and arrogance. Thus, it will never supersede what humans already know about themselves. What science does not realize is that the most defining concepts in the universe do not fit in a logical box of linearity. **They can't; they are quantum, they are multidimensional**, as is the planet and everything in it.